less sticky than a Band-Aid

faster-acting than time-release capsules

easier to swallow than chalky pills

no child-proof cap necessary

Dr. Amelia's Boredom Survival Guide

better-tasting than that nasty cough syrup

GLOR GRU SYR

First Aid for Rainy Days, Boring Errands, Waiting Rooms, Whatever!

by Marissa Moss

(and Dr. Amelia, brain surgeon)

no thermometer required

American Girl

IN CASE OF EMERGENCY

TURN PAGE

This guide is
dedicated, with great
excitement, to
Brion,
who practically never gets bored.

Are you bored enough to bother to read this? Then you really need this guide!

Pleasant Company
Publications
8400 Fairway Place
Middleton, Wisconsin 53562

Book Design by Amelia

Library of Congress Cataloging-in-Publication Data
Moss, Marissa
Dr. Amelia's boredom survival guide: first aid for rainy days,
boring errands, waiting rooms, whatever!/by Marissa Moss
p. cm.
"American Girl."
Summary: While waiting for her sister's medical appointment,
a bored Amelia creates a handwritten book of fifty suggestions
for passing the time.
ISBN 1-56247-794-3 (pbk.)
I. American Girl (Middleton, Wis.)   II. Title.
PZ7.M8535 Dr 1999   98-54758
[Fic] -- dc21   CIP
                                        AC

haven't you forgotten someone?

First Pleasant Company Publications printing, 1999

An Amelia™ Book
American Girl™ is a trademark of Pleasant Company.
Amelia™ and the black-and-white notebook pattern
are trademarks of Marissa Moss.

Manufactured in Singapore

Prevent Tedium Foot 124

Is this part of a jump rope rhyme?

00 01 02 03 04 TWP 10 9 8 7 6 5 4 3

Why do doctors never see you when you come on time for an appointment? You *always* have to wait! Why don't they just tell you to come later?

← regular clock

doctor's clock →

Doctors have their own time zone.

I didn't have to go to the doctor, Cleo did (probably for an ingrown pimple — yucch!), but Mom dragged me along anyway, so here I am, stuck in this waiting room with *nothing* to do.

I forgot to bring a book, but at least I have this little notebook to write in. Or I could read a magazine...

Waiting room magazines are always at least three years old and they're on the ~~weirdest~~ ~~wierdest~~ weirdest subjects.

↑ at last!

AMERICAN TEETH
Your Gums and You
FLOSS
GUM OR GUMS?

DECOUPAGE TODAY
BLAH BLAH
TURN POSTCARDS INTO ART
PAGES PACKED WITH

OBOE DIGEST

Or I could play with the box of decrepit, broken baby toys.

doll missing an eye — like a bad advertisement for the doctor →

← stiff hair — mostly bald

real underwear with genuine holes →

xylophone with no hammer ↓

could be used as a sled for the doll, I guess ↑

3 building blocks ↓

see how tall a tower you can make! ↑

I'M BORED!

All right, I've had it! Since there's nothing here for me, I'll <u>make</u> something. I'll make a guide of 50 fun, cool things to do, so if I'm ever stuck in a boring place like this again, I'll have my handy-dandy guide to rely on.

Potential Boring Situations

at grown-up parties ↓

yada yada yada

blah blah blah blah

when I'm sent to my room ↓

DO NOT ENTER

SLAM!

when I'm stuck in traffic

Are we there yet?

MAKING FACES

Thing to Do #1
See if you can touch the tip of your nose with your tongue.

↑ use a mirror!

Thing to Do #2
Try to wiggle your ears and eyebrows at the same time.

↑ fake eyebrows don't count

Thing to Do #3
Practice winking.

This is as close as I can get — I just can't wink!

Time used up: A wink in time saves nine.

Thinking of Nadia gave me this idea. She has the loooooongest tongue I've ever seen — she can lick ice cream off her chin!

Try to look cross-eyed, but not for too long or your eyes will get stuck that way (says Mom).

Look, Ma, no hands!

TONGUE TO-DO'S

Thing to Do #4

Now that your tongue is warmed up, make some tongue twisters and say them as fast as you can.

mmblgm

↑ tongue knot

Here's some I invented:

"Clunky Cleo crawled and clawed into claustrophobic caves."

piles of peach, prune, and pecan pie →

← perky, peppy pig pacers

"Pink pigs prance prettily past plenty of prune pie."

Time used up: However long it takes before your tongue gets numb.

Carly has the fastest tongue in the West — no one says "faster!" "She sells seashells down by the seashore"

NOISES PAGE

↑ oops! <u>not</u> noses – <u>noises</u>!

Thing to Do #5

Try to make as many noises as you can without using your voice, like snapping your fingers, drumming them on the table, tapping your toes, popping your cheek with your finger. Are you driving people crazy yet? Then STOP IT!

WARNING: Make <u>these</u> noises only when no one else is around or no one will <u>ever</u> want to be around you.

Thing to Do #6 ←

Enough annoying noises – now try to make gross noises. Burp as loud as you can, suck your teeth, smack your lips, snort.

nubby waiting room carpet ↓

knocked flat by a <u>powerful</u> BURP! ↓

Time used up: Depends on how much grossness you can take.

..ₒBUUUURRPP   If you guessed this is Cleo's favorite activity, you're RIGHT!

drip drip

tip tap tip tap

clip clop clip clop

SOUND EFFECTS

Thing to Do #7
   Think up comic book sound effects for
real life. (I mean, who uses BIF!
and WHAM! ?)

I got this idea from Maya — she loves to read comic books.

when you blow a
wrapper off a
straw

THWIP

fwish!

SMOOF!

↑
when you spit out
toothpaste

↑
when you plop down on an
armchair or a sofa

Time used up: Holy fish sticks, Batman,
it's time for GAWOOMMMPKAA!

E Y E T R I C K S

Thing to Do #8

Stare hard at something — a lamp, a doorknob, a chair leg. Stare until you see two of whatever it is. Try to make the two things one again. Now two again. Now one.

If you can't make yourself see double, see how long you can stare without blinking.

Time used up: Until your eyes see triple.

Which lamp is the real one?

Made ya blink!

Mom says that if it is bad for your eyes, She just likes to rhyme and say, "Eyes are made to use, not to abuse!" — the Mom warning finger — beware!

Answer: None. These are all drawings of lamps. Gotcha!

JUST LOOKING, THANKS

Thing to Do #9

Make the cracks in the ceiling into pictures, like you do with clouds. Find a dragon, a cat, a secret message. *If the ceiling is made of that ugly speckled tile, skip this and rate the room down 2 points in Thing to Do #12.*

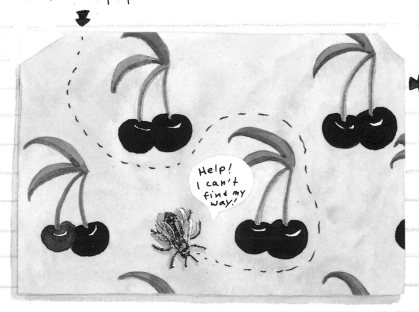

Thing to Do #10

If there's wallpaper, make a path on it with your eyes — create a wallpaper maze! But don't get lost or your eyes will be stuck looking at that wallpaper forever!

Leah likes to pretend she's a spy and has to memorize all the details in the room because <u>something</u> is a bomb in disguise.

Veeeery interesting!

magnifying glass

Help! I can't find my way!

← Paintings that look like a 2-year-old did them get a −10 score

← little lamp attached to frame as if the picture belonged in a museum — deduct 5 points

Thing to Do #11

Balance pennies (or other coins) on the baseboard. See how many you can line up. If you want to get fancy and you have a lot of different coins, make a pattern or pretend the faces are talking to each other.

Thing to Do #12

Rate the room you're in from 1 to 10, 1 being the ugliest, 10 the most beautiful.

Deduct 2 points if the rug is an unnameable color (like pinkish-brownish-yellowish).

Deduct 1 point for every picture that looks the same upside down as right-side up.

Time used up: Lemme out of this room — I've spent waaay too much time in here!

↖ oops! It's hung upside down!

Thing to Do #13

   Don't do anything at all! Thirteen is
an unlucky number, so just skip it!

Time used up: The time it took you
to read this page.

EEEEK! The curse
of 13 is spreading!

Don't even touch this page. It's full of BAD LUCK! Oh, no — too late!

13

FORTUNE TELLING

Thing to Do #14
  List all the superstitions you can think of,
like how some buildings have no 13th floor—
so the elevator goes from the 12th floor right
to the 14th floor.

Did you ever wonder why a dozen is 12, not 13? Why people have 10 fingers and not 13? Why high school only goes to 12th grade? Now you know!

Time used up: Seven years of bad luck.

VISUAL DICTIONARY of SUPERSTITIONS

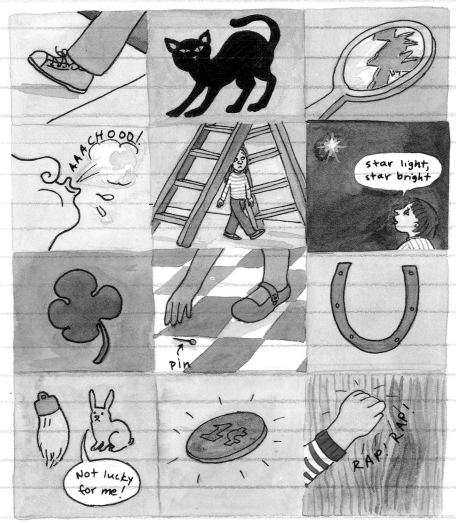

Match the superstition with the picture: Wishing on a star, Four-leaf clover, Black cat, See a pin and pick it up and all day long you'll have good luck, Knock on wood, Step on a crack and break your mother's back, Walking under a ladder, Finding a penny, Saying "Bless you" when somebody sneezes, Horseshoe, Rabbit's foot, Break a mirror and get seven years' bad luck.

GOOD 🍀 LUCK

Thing to Do #15
 Are you lucky? Take the following quiz
to see how lucky you are.

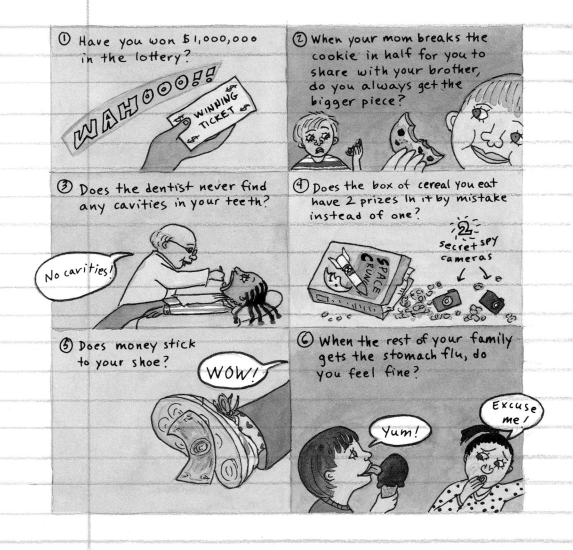

good luck– yay!

bad luck. oh no! →

If you said yes to all 6: You are the luckiest person alive!

If you said yes to 5: You should definitely buy a lottery ticket.

If you said yes to 4: You should invest in the stock market when you grow up.

If you said yes to 3: You are one lucky dog, you!

If you said yes to 2: You are still pretty lucky.

If you said yes to 1: You need to find a four-leaf clover.

If you said yes to 0: You are beyond hope. Don't bother with a good luck charm.

Time used up: If you're lucky, all of it.

BAD LUCK

Thing to Do #16
Are you unlucky? Take the following test to see how unlucky you are.

If you said yes to 0: Buy a lottery ticket. You may be lucky!

If you said yes to 1: You need to make sure your lucky horseshoe isn't upside down by mistake.

If you said yes to 2: Don't make a bet with your friend — no way you'll win.

If you said yes to 3: Stay away from sharp objects.

If you said yes to 4: Stay inside with the drapes drawn.

If you said yes to 5: You poor devil, you.

If you said yes to 6: Get away from me — quick!

Time used up: If you're unlucky, it's already too late.

drops her toast buttered-side down.

...very unlucky — this unlucky — someone who always

FINGER PLAY

↑ or If you have markers or pencils with you, you can always color your fingernails.

Thing to Do #17

  Pretend your hand is an animal. Walk it around the room. Give it a name, like Pinky or Finger Frances. Now make both your hands into animals and let them play together. They can climb furniture, race each other, dance, tickle, or argue.

Time used up: This can go on for a long while if you have a lot of imagination, and your finger pets have a lot to say.

That kid who always waves his hands around a lot, Eli — I saw him doing this at recess. It was hilarious!

Thing to Do #18
   If there's a lamp or strong enough
sunlight, make shadow puppets. Try
to think of new ways to use your hands,
new kinds of shapes you can make.

practice rabbit
ears or play little
Bunny Foo Foo

make a beaky
dragon

make a cup
shadow and
drink out of it

Or use your whole body and make strange
creatures.

a rare
two-legged
elephant

Time used up: In the snap of a finger.

FACE FUN

Thing to Do #19
   Draw freckles on your face with marker.
(Make sure it's the washable kind!) Now connect
the dots. See any constellations on your
cheeks? If you already have freckles, don't
bother to draw new ones, just connect
the ones you have.

Time used up: Depending on how freckly you
are and how complicated you make your
constellations, a good spot of time.

WRONG!
↓

permanent
marker
↙

RIGHT!
↙

washable
marker →

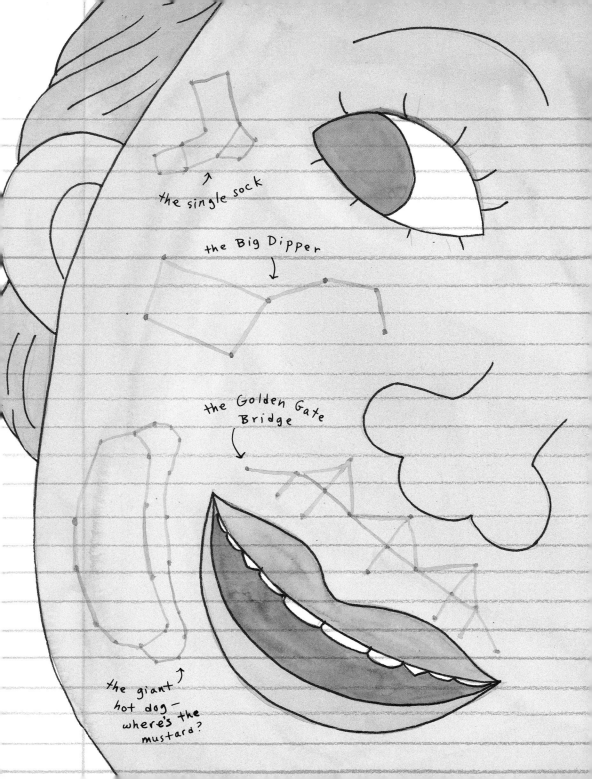

KNOW YOURSELF

Thing to Do #20

How well do you know yourself? Take this quiz and find out! (No fair checking before you answer.)

Count the number of correct answers.

If you answered all 6 correctly: Congratulations! You are an expert on yourself.

If you answered 5 correctly: Very good — not even your mother knows you _this_ well.

If you answered 4 correctly: Not bad, but you'd better spend more time with yourself.

If you answered 3 correctly: Open your eyes! Pay attention to yourself!

If you answered 2 correctly: Careful — do you want to be a stranger to yourself?

If you answered 1 correctly: You _are_ a stranger to yourself!

If you answered 0 correctly: Better introduce yourself to yourself!

Time used up: You have your whole life to figure yourself out.

Cleo's best friend, Gigi, is always reading self-help books, but Cleo's the one who _needs_ them.

Are You a Secret Snorer? by D. Nose

self-help guides

How to Find the Real You! (Look in the yellow pages) by Hyde N. seek

WORD GAMES

Thing to Do #21

Make up your own alphabet. Make letters that look different and have different names than plain old ABC's.

the letter tzeek

the letter goomph

the letter mitta

Oops! This is just an electrical outlet!

Repeat after me, class.

And I don't mean cross words. (What, me angry?)

Time used up: Depends on how many letters your alphabet has.

Thing to Do #22

Make up brand-new words of your own to replace ordinary, already-used words, like "bummitchel" for "bored." Then when the doctor asks, "How are you today?" you say, "I'm bummitchel!"

My carnoople is especially blatcha today.

Translation: My sister is especially grouchy today.

Like my teacher, Ms. Busby, says, "You can't flamdoodle me!"

Time used up: About snargle minutes.

Thing to Do #23

Say a word over and over again until it doesn't sound like it means anything anymore. It's just a noise.

Nose. Nose. Nose. Nose. Nose. Nose. Nose. Nose. Nose. Nose. Nose. Nose. Nose. Nose. Nose. Nose.

Time used up: Time. Time. Time. Time. Time. Time. What does "time" mean again?

The Gradual Deterioration of a Nose

A Nose Becomes a Noise

I have to give my old teacher, Mr. Nudel, credit for this one. His name made me think of it. Nudel. Noodle. Nudel. Noodel. Nudel. Noodel. Nudle. Noodel. Nudell. Noodell.

RHYME TIME

Thing to Do #24
Think of new, funny ways to end this rhyme:

"Roses are red,
Violets are blue..."

animal endings
(tails to you)

Possible Endings:

"Sugar is sticky
And so are you!"

match the ending
to the
beginning

"Sheep go baa
And Cows go moo."

"Almonds are nuts
And so are you."

"I call it a bathroom,
You call it a loo."

Where is it?

I feel so naked without my tail!

mad →

I don't mean that kind of expression!

EXPRESSIONS

scared ↑

Thing to Do #25

Think up all the figures of speech you can, like, for example:

"making a monkey out of me"

"using elbow grease"

"walking on eggshells"

"putting your nose to the grindstone"

"walking on air"

"mad as a wet hen"

"happy as a lark"

"between a rock and a hard place"

Draw pictures of what these expressions make you think of — this is the fun part!

This is like Mrs. Kravitz, the music teacher. She says oddball expressions all the time, like "It's no use crying over spilled lemonade."

Time used up: There's no time like the present.

Now!

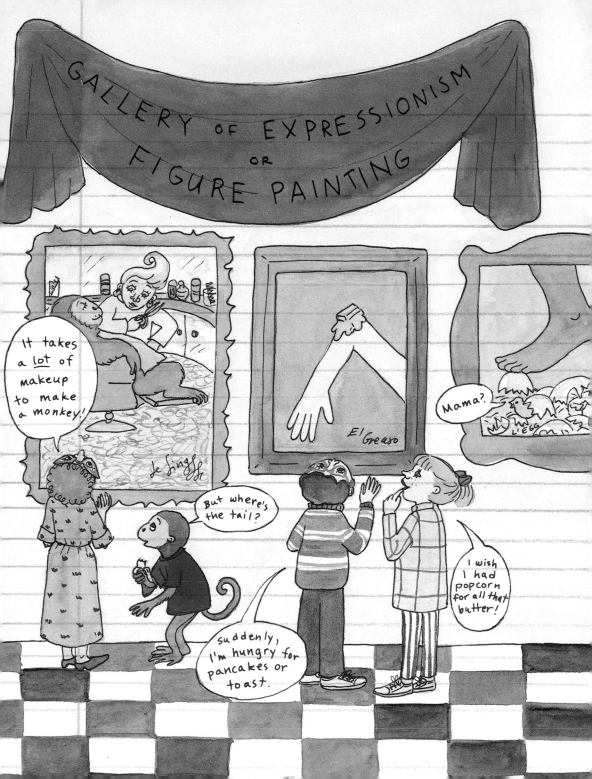

Thing to Do #26

If you were good at Thing to Do #25, you'll be great at this! Think up all the expressions you can that have to do with your body.

For example:

"batting your eyelashes"

"a stomach tied in knots"

"eyes in the back of your head"

"making your skin crawl"

"cutting off your nose to spite your face"

"a broken heart"

Try drawing pictures of these. It should be pretty interesting.

Time used up: Time to wake up and smell the coffee.

Ms. Jenko, the P.E. teacher, uses these kinds of expressions, like "Put your heart into it" or "It's mind over matter." When she wants us to listen, she says, "Now kids, I want you to be all ears." I can't help thinking of Mr. Potato Head with ears in all the holes.

TWEEET

Mr. Potato "All Ears" Head

Make Your Own Fortune

Thing to Do #27

   Here's a chance to invent your <u>own</u>
expressions. Make up sayings to go
into fortune cookies.

Good things happen to those who write their own fortunes.

A cookie in need is a cookie indeed.

Those who eat fortune cookies make crumbs.

A fortune awaits you (in a cookie!).

I see... orange Pekoe!

Cleo reading tea leaves

Time used up: As long as it takes for the
cookie to crumble.

crumbs — yum!
↓

Important Somebody

Thing to Do #28
    Design your own business cards.
Make them for your family and friends,

My card!

Amelia
notebook writer
extraordinaire
(and pretty good artist)

Mrs. Kravitz ♪
Music Teacher

"Always keeping the beat." ♪♫

Jelly Roll Nose
ⁿ C L E O ⊂
Professional Pain—
in-the-You-Know-
Where
12 years' experience

M ○ M
chauffeur · cook · cleaner ·
shopper · bookkeeper ·
homework helper · errand
runner · secretary · laundress ·
gardener · letter writer · etc.

SINGSONG

Thing to Do #29

   Make up your own jump rope songs.
Use tunes you know, or make up the
tune, too.

Carly is the jump rope expert, especially in Double Dutch.

Down by the tetherball,
Down by Room One,
Johnny traded peanut
   butter
For an old bun.
He opened wide
To take a bite.
How many molars did
   Johnny lose?
One, two, three. . .

Porcupine, Porcupine,
Your sock has a hole.
Porcupine, Porcupine,
Stick out your toe.
Porcupine, Porcupine,
Those quills are like spikes!
Porcupine, Porcupine,
Yikes, yikes, yikes!

Time used up: Not last
night, but the night before.

Maya is good, too.

WORLD GAMES

Thing to Do #30

Make a map of the world. If you're not sure what country is where, make up your own.

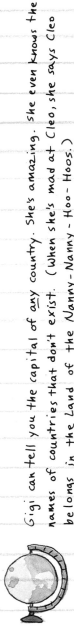

Gigi can tell you the capital of any country. She's amazing. She even knows the names of countries that don't exist. (When she's mad at Cleo, she says Cleo belongs in the Land of the Nanny-Nanny-Hoo-Hoos.)

Time used up: Pacific standard time, Greenwich mean time, daylight saving time.

wiener dog flag ↗

Thing to Do #31
   Design flags to go with your countries, or make new flags to replace the ones countries already have.

JELLY BEAN-LAND

TIC-TAC-TOE-LAND

OVER THE RAINBOW-LAND

REALLY FREEZING-LAND

Time used up: International time.

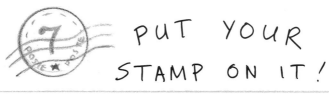

PUT YOUR
STAMP ON IT!

Thing to Do #32

Design your own postage stamp collection.
What or who would you like to see
commemorated on a stamp?

Draw your own!

birthday cakes
of the rich and
famous ↘

favorite teddy bears ↗

↖ snazzy swimming pools

designer socks ↗

Mako, my Japanese pen pal, sent me some great stamps on his letters, so I thought I'd make my own.

Time used up: You know how slow the post office is!

Great Vegetables I Have Known
(but not necessarily eaten)

IT'S GOOD
❀ FOR YOU ❀

CORN ON THE COB
10¢   mmmm!

TOE-MAY-TOE
3¢

83¢
TOE-MAH-TOE

20¢
PEA·PEA·PEA

18¢
Have you ever seen a carrot wear glasses?

Grown-ups Famous for Distinguishing
Features

31¢
AUNT BEA—
BAD BREATH!

THE LARGE MOLE
SUBSTITUTE TEACHER
12¢

SHARP NAILS
CAFETERIA LADY   7¢

THE DENTIST
16¢
HAIRY NOSTRILS

Dogs of the Neighborhood

SPARKY
15¢

BUTCH
6¢

10¢ sausage 10¢

DOG WITH EAR MUFFINS
LULU
5¢

FOOD FOR THOUGHT

Thing to Do #33:
Make a list of good foods and gross foods. Post it on the refrigerator when you're finished so your mom or dad will know what to make for dinner.

YES! MAKE IT! GOOD!	NO! Forget About It! BAD!
pizza	liver
spaghetti	green beans
french fries	peas
baked potato	brussels sprouts
grilled cheese	anchovies
corn on the cob	sardines
biscuits	any fish
mashed potato	any pudding with funny
pie	little bumps in it, like
ice cream	tapioca (tapiyuccha)—
muffins	don't even try it!
cookies	onions
cupcakes	anything that's runny
	and gooey-looking
	like raw egg—
	yucch!

Time used up: Enough time to make a tasty batch of cookies.

There's this kid at school, Melissa, who says there are no nasty foods, but then, she'll eat anything. She loves cafeteria food, even Mystery Mush.

Mystery Mush— part stew, part dog food

Thing to Do #34
   Using foods only from your good list (of course),
draw a menu of your idea of the PERFECT meal.
Use this as a hint for the cook in your house.

Le Café Chez Me!

~ appetizer ~
cheesy crackers (no stinky
cheeses — first choice is the kind
that comes out of a can)

~ salad ~

Jell-O with marshmallows
(yes, this counts as a green
salad if it's lime Jell-O)

↑ wiggling the
Jell-O is permitted

~ main ~
dish

pizza, spaghetti, or
   fried chicken
   (french fries are
       optional)

↑ all can be eaten
with fingers —
even the
spaghetti;

~ dessert ~

ice cream sundae with
fudge sauce, whipped cream,
and a maraschino cherry

↙ Six flavors is just fine!

Time used up: Dinner time!

SCIENTIFIC EXPERIMENTS
without test tubes!

Thing to Do #35
   Pretend your room is a paleological dig
and you are excavating for fossils.
Carefully label your finds. (This will
work in the car, too.)

protective
cotton
↓

Petrified Pretzel

Fossilized
Cheerio

Prehistoric Puzzle
Piece

tissue
↓

Bug Preserved
in Amber of
Ancient
Lollipop

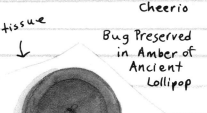

Lump of Dried-Out
Play-Doh
Pressed Flat in Sedimentary
Layers of Sheets and Blankets

Time used up: Eons and eons.

Is your
room
clean?

This one is in honor of my mom, who is always threatening to
carbon-date the socks under my bed.

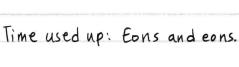

Thing to Do #36
   Pretend you are an alien from another planet. Try to describe your surroundings and what earthlings are like to your fellow aliens.

Time used up: Light years.

SCIENCE IN ACTION

Thing to Do #37

Design useful inventions, like an automatic clothes-folder or a pill you can chew instead of brushing your teeth.

Cleo Alarm

INTRUDER ALERT

↑ clip onto your pocket; light flashes yellow when Cleo enters range — when she is _really_ near, light turns red and beeping sound warns you — BEWARE!

Miracle Food Additive

YUCCH TO YUM
TASTE TRANSFORMER

One drop of this amazing formula turns any gross food into a good food. Presto-chango! Broccoli becomes brownies, liver becomes lasagna, and mushrooms become maraschino cherries.

I'm done, Mom.

De-Raisiner

↑

Is your oatmeal ruined by wrinkly raisins? Do you want to remove unsightly dried fruit from your cookies? Then this is the invention for you!

Is your mom mad at you? Are you about to be sent to your room? Never fear! Mood Softener is here! Spray gently in front of the angry parent and within seconds, you'll be offered a special treat!

↓

Go to your room, young lady!

Want to get some ice cream?

before ↗

Mood Softener

↖ after

creative time-keeping

Time used up: Invent a new kind of clock! Make your own time system — why be stuck with hours and minutes when you can have churkas and loomies?

PENCIL POWER

Thing to Do #38

Think of great first sentences for a story. Then think of the rest of the story.

① "Oh, no!" Jones shouted as she stepped into the room.

② The drums were beating steadily, a bad sign for sure.

③ There was no question that this was the largest bug Alfred had ever seen.

④ It's not easy to stuff a suitcase with 62 jars of cranberry jelly, but that's just what Shirley did.

⑤ The clouds boiled in the pot of sky.

Time used up: Once upon a time.

Leah and I took turns writing a story this way. It was a lot of fun. And we ended up with a pretty good tale.

Thing to Do #39
  Do the same thing for cartoons. Draw
several first panels for a comic strip. Then
go back and draw what comes next.

Time used up: Later that day...

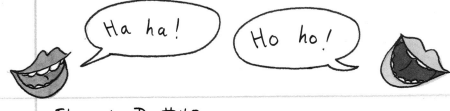

Thing to Do #40
   Think of all the knock-knock jokes you know. Tell them to yourself if you can't find anyone to tell them to.

Knock, knock.

Who's there?

Noenny.

Noenny who?

Noenny good knock-knock jokes?

Knock, knock.   Who's there?
Thar she.   Thar she who?
Thar she blows, Jelly Roll Nose!

for you, Cleo! →

Time used up: Knock, knock.   Who's there?
             Howlongs.   Howlongs who?
             Howlongs this gonna take?

What's an undercover store?

Where you buy a bed!

Thing to Do #41

Have some pun! Get it? That's a pun — pun, fun — get it? Okay, you got it. Now make up some puns of your own. Draw pictures to go with them.

Ms. Bussly is the Queen of Puns. She doesn't tell a lot of jokes, but she loves puns.

Bald man's motto: "Hair today, gone tomorrow."

DANGER: RADIATION

Gone Fission

Sign on atomic scientist's door

Did you hear about the eager potato?

It's all eyes!

What does the butcher say to her customers? "Pleased to meat you!"

Time used up: What time did the kid go to the dentist? Two-thirty. (Tooth-hurty!)

Thing to Do #42
  Now that you're in a punny mood, make up cute business names, ones that are puns or jokes, like a pet store called "The Doggy in the Window" or a hair salon called "Shear Delight."

Bakery called "You Take the Cake"

Indian café called "Delhi Deli"

Pizza place called "Pie in the Sky"

Is this a shoe size or a battery?

SIZE 10 AAAA

Shoe store called "If the Shoe Fits, Wear It"

Did you hear about the electronics store?

It's called "Batteries Included!"

Time used up: A portable-clock store called "Tick Tock Tote."

Name That Face!

Thing to Do #43:

  Give a new name to everyone in your family. Then try to find the perfect name for your friends. Think of names that <u>really</u> fit their personalities. (Some people might <u>already</u> have names that are exactly like who they are — like me, Amelia!)

> I'm waaaa-aaaiting!

Cleo really acts and looks like a Bertha — she even <u>sounds</u> like a Bertha (especially when she burps!).

Mom's real name is Patience — something she definitely does not have a lot of. Her name should be Enid or Roxanne.

Time used up: A minute by any other name would last as long.

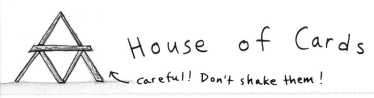

House of Cards

← careful! Don't shake them!

Thing to Do #44

Design your own deck of cards. Then play War with yourself. Or 52-Card Pickup. Make up your own card game and give it a great name, like Lucky Fours, Doodle, or Thumbkin.

Time used up: Time for Crazy Eights, Spit, Hearts, Casino, Gin Rummy, Fish, Seven Card Stud, Five Card Draw, Twenty-One, Honeymoon Bridge, Canasta, Solitaire, Old Maid, Pinochle, Idiot, and WAR!

Veeery interesting!

3 of Cupcakes

4 of Cheese

9 of Yo Yos

Deuce of Toothbrushes

Ace of Peanut Butter

8 of Eyeglasses

Queen of Dalmatians

10 of Socks

6 of Lemons

7 of Crayons

Jack of Dragons

5 of Ice Cream Cones

CERTIFICATE for SURVIVING BOREDOM

Thing to Do #45
   Make certificates for your family and friends.
Think about what each person does especially
well.

Nadia got an award for best story at the Young Authors Fair, but I've never gotten an award for anything!

This Award Certifies That

Leah

is the best, neatest underwear
folder in the world

For Faithful and Frequent
Letter Writing
the highly coveted
Blue Ribbon Stamp
Award
to
Nadia

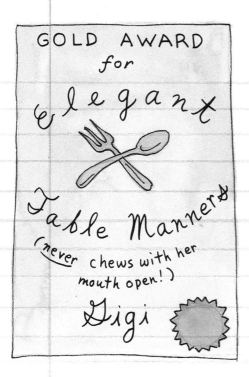

GOLD AWARD
for
elegant

Table Manners
(never chews with her
mouth open!)
Gigi

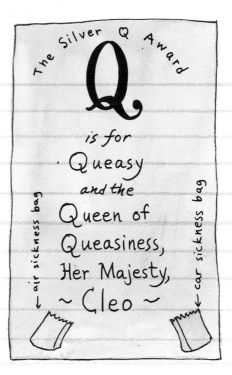

The Silver Q Award

Q

is for
• Queasy
and the
Queen of
Queasiness,
Her Majesty,
~ Cleo ~

← air sickness bag

car sickness bag →

The
Double Jump-Rope
Certificate
Best Double Dutch Rope Jumper
Carly

Time used up: Time to present an award!
(Think up a good toast to go with it.)

Thing to Do #46

OK, you've designed business cards, menus, and award certificates — now here's your chance to design your own OLYMPICS! What events would you include? Now try training for each event. (And think of the snazzy athletic wear to go with each sport.)

For example:

Popcorn Toss

The athlete needs nerves of steel and keen concentration. A second of inattention means the popcorn hits the floor — or worse yet, your forehead — instead of your mouth.

For extra credit, design the gold, silver, and bronze medals to go with each event.

gold medal for Popcorn Toss

Judges consider the height of the popcorn's flight when giving out the scores.

Chair-Spinning

A sense of balance, keen reflexes, and most important, a stomach that isn't easily queasy are essential in this sport. The athlete must spin as long as possible without getting miserably dizzy. The faster the spin, the higher the score.

after a successful spin →

← note the fashionable spin-suit

Floor — Sliding

A good, slippery waxed floor and some socks are all the equipment necessary. The length of the slide matters most, but style and speed also count.

← setting a record!

Time used up: Every four years.

Thing to Do # 47

Now it's time for some mental Olympics with the Total Trivia Quiz. See how well you do.

If you got 0 right: You're just an average
person with no interest in the details around you.

If you got 1 right: You are not very observant.
Better check to see if your fly is zipped.

If you got 2 right: Not bad — maybe you just
need to open your eyes wider.

If you got 3 right: You are sensitive to the
finer things in life.

If you got 4 right: You are very perceptive
and have a sharp mind.

If you got 5 right: You can easily earn a
Ph.D. in Trivia — congratulations!

If you got 6 right: You're a genius! Can I
have your autograph?

If you got 7 right: Hey, you cheated!
. (Or you didn't even notice how many
questions there are.)

Time used up! Time to pay attention!

sharp eyes noticing everything!

MORE MAPS

Thing to Do #48
 Draw a diagram of your brain. Label all the relevant parts.

Thing to Do #49
 Make a map of your heart. Label each section.
Time used up: In a heartbeat!

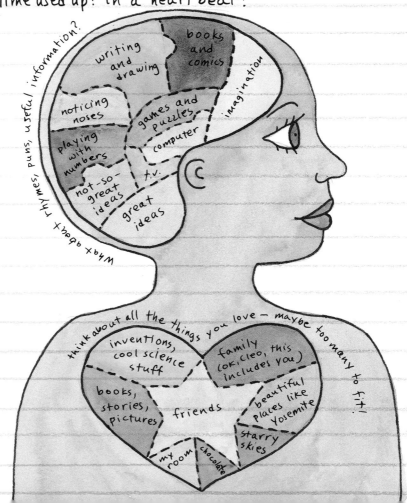

See, Mr. Nudel, I'm using my noodle!

Thing to Do #50
   You know those notebooks with the Tables of
Useful Information on the back cover? Here's
your chance to make your own Useful Information
Page. Think of all those things you really want
to know.

Table of Mom Minutes

"In a minute" when she's cooking   =   20 minutes
"In a minute" when she's reading =   15 minutes
"In a minute" when she's in the shower = 30 minutes
"In a minute" when she's on the phone =   2 hours

Measure of Doctor's Idea of Pain

"This won't hurt a bit." =   it will hurt a little
"Now, this is just going to sting." = it will hurt a lot
"It will all be over in a second." = YEOUCH!

Time used up: A mom minute. (Yes, but which
one?)

I can't believe it — just as I finish this guide, before I have a chance to actually USE it, here comes Cleo. Wouldn't you know it! Now we have to go, and I can't do any of the cool things I wrote down.

Oh well, maybe I'll get lucky and there'll be a big traffic jam. I'll be ready!